WALKING THE ROMAN WA~ ~

Hadrian's Wall has greeted a long line of vis including William Camden, John Horsley, William Stu - and old William Hutton of Birmingham, who, in 18(*miles to see a shattered Wall.* It was in June 1849 that th the Roman Wall took place, when the Rev. Dr. Johi ~g~~~~ ~~~~~ escorted a party of pilgrims, as they were called, from Wallsend-on-Tyne to Bowness-on-Solway. The popular appeal of this antiquarian ramble led Richard Abbatt, one of the pilgrims, to write a memoir called *The Picts or Romano-British Wall.* In 1851, Dr. Bruce published the first edition of *The Roman Wall.* The third edition of 1867 was a large quarto volume and its 466 pages included many fine lithographs and engravings. In 1875, Henry Irwin Jenkinson published his *Practical Guide to the Roman Wall and neighbourhood.* In 1886, the ageing Dr. Bruce led the Second Pilgrimage of the Roman Wall, inspiring a tradition that has continued every ten years. In 1888, W. W. Tomlinson outlined the course of the Wall between Newcastle and Greenhead in his *Comprehensive Guide to Northumberland.*

Walking the Wall was not just for the gentlemen. In 1908, Maria Hoyer published her notes on a summer holiday in a book called *By the Roman Wall.* In 1922, Jessie Mothersole, a talented and much-travelled artist, published her *Hadrian's Wall.* The first edition contained an invitation to the London exhibition of the 25 water-colours intended for her book. For the ordinary visitor, Hugh Lanaway had produced a pocket-guide entitled *A Holiday Ramble along the Great Wall in the North.* It could be bought for sixpence from the George Hotel at Chollerford.

In 1926, Professor R. G. Collingwood published two pocket-guides, one for the Chesters Museum and the other for the Roman Wall. This gave advice on access and lodgings and aimed to give the visitor *all he need know in a shape that will not burden anyone's pocket or knapsack, and at a price that will not add appreciably to the cost of the most economically-planned visit.* In 1929, the Newcastle Society of Antiquaries produced a penny pamphlet called *The Roman Wall and How to Reach it.* This suggested an itinerary for the visitor with only a day or two to see the Wall.

The increasing number of visitors coincided with a period of great upheaval. Much of the land around Hadrian's Wall changed hands in June 1929, with the sale of 20,000 acres of the Chesters estate, the legacy of John Clayton (1792-1890). He owned most of the finest parts of the Roman Wall and five Roman forts, including Chesters and Housesteads. On 3rd January 1930, Mr. J. M. Clayton presented Housesteads fort and 3/4 mile of Roman Wall to the National Trust. Professor G. M. Trevelyan bought Housesteads farm, which had failed to reach its reserve price. He later gave the land for Housesteads museum. This opened on 23rd July 1936 - in torrential rain. It cost £800 and was built out of the sixpences paid by visitors to the fort. On 31st December 1930, *The Times* announced that Mr. J. M. Clayton had given the Clayton Collection of Roman Antiquities to a body of trustees. One of these was Captain A. M. Keith, the new owner of Chesters, who promoted access to the fort and museum. Admission was sixpence or one shilling, depending on the day of the week. The original tickets sported four small swastikas, an ancient symbol of good luck. Mr. Eric Birley, an eminent scholar, acquired Chesterholm and began to excavate the fort of Vindolanda. The Roman forts at Carrawburgh and Carvoran remained under grass. Threats to extend quarrying along the Roman Wall were repelled.

Public transport had put the Roman Wall within the reach of ordinary people. Around 1930, Robert Emmerson & Co., who ran *The Connecting Link* bus service between Newcastle and Carlisle, produced an illustrated booklet called *The Road of the Roman*, in which John Gibson, a talented photographer and local historian, described the Roman Wall and other places of interest between the two cities. This route remains one of the longest in England.

In 1931, Robert Hugill published his *Road Guide to Northumberland and the Border*. Extolling the delights of the open road, this book recognised the increasing use of private transport and contained 35 routes with 41 maps and plans. Route 29 described the Roman Wall in some detail. In 1932, Paul Brown published an illustrated book of popular appeal entitled *The Great Wall of Hadrian in Roman Times*. He later produced *The Road to Housesteads*, a pamphlet that described a drive along the Military Road from Newcastle to Housesteads, where the Wall-hungry pilgrim would receive *sermons in stones* from the Roman remains.

In his book, published in 1936 and entitled *Walking Tours and Hostels in England*, Sydney Moorhouse outlined a four-day tour of the Roman Wall, using the new Youth Hostels at Once Brewed and Acomb. The book had a message from Professor G. M. Trevelyan, the first president of the Youth Hostels Association, who had made a personal donation for the building of the Once Brewed. In 1938, a year after W. P. Collier died, Alfred Wainwright, later renowned for his pictorial guides to the Lakeland Fells, spent a fortnight on a walking tour from Settle, covering the Roman Wall from lodgings in Hexham and Haltwhistle - and penning the wistful thoughts that he published as *A Pennine Journey* almost 50 years later.

The classic guide remains the *Handbook to the Roman Wall*, first published as the *Wallet-Book* in 1863 by John Collingwood Bruce. Three editions of the Handbook, with several reprints, appeared during the career of W. P. Collier. The 13th edition, revised and extended by Charles Daniels, was published in 1978.

Writers often mention the people they met on their travels but admit that communication could be a problem. John Archer published his *Artist's Ramble along the line of the Picts' Wall* in 1861 and promised the visitor *matter for amusement, and even instruction, in the manners and dialect of the people, with whom he will make acquaintance.* James Wardell published his *Tour along the Roman Wall* in 1862 and recalls what happened when he and his friend visited Housesteads. Heavy rain had forced them to seek shelter at the farm. *We were asked if we would have a 'glass of Roman water.' My friend, misunderstanding the northern pronunciation, thought the man said 'rum and water' and very eagerly accepted his offer. I was much amused at his surprise, when a bucket was let down into a well in front of the house, lined with Roman masonry, and brought to the surface filled with sparkling water, of which a glass was handed to us.*

It is fitting that this book should include two portraits of Thomas Thompson (1850-1938). This fine figure of a man, over six feet tall and broad in proportion, with a white beard and moustache, was both the custodian of Housesteads fort and one of its main attractions. *Many distinguished visitors have from time to time chatted with him on his domain and, even when they could not understand all that he said, were struck by his fine bearing and his obvious affection for the treasures of which he was the guardian.*

A collection of books on Hadrian's Wall would fill the shelves of a small library, not counting the articles that have appeared in the volumes of the local learned societies. In his scholarly survey, *Research on Hadrian's Wall*, published in 1961, Professor Eric Birley listed over 500 names connected with the Roman Wall and the list has grown longer every year. As visitors to the Roman Wall, whether scholars or tourists, we all have something of the pilgrim in us as we follow in the footsteps of thousands who have gone before. We come, we see, we ponder. *Sic transit gloria muri.*

THE GEORGE HOTEL   This picture was probably taken shortly after the death of its genial landlord, James Simmonds, in May 1921. *From morning to night in fine weather, his tall figure and cheery face, crowned with white hair, were to be seen outside the George, where he held himself ready to extend a welcome to all.* With its riverside gardens, the George has always been a special place for visitors to the Roman Wall, including George Bernard Shaw and Rudyard Kipling. The extended Swallow George Hotel now has 47 bedrooms, a fine restaurant, a full range of conference facilities and a leisure centre.

FOUNDATION OF ROMAN BRIDGE AT CHOLLERFORD 70

CHESTERS BRIDGE A path from Chollerford Bridge leads to the remains of two Roman bridges. The first carried Hadrian's Wall alone across the River North Tyne. Most of the visible remains belong to the abutment of a second bridge, built about 80 years later, which carried the Wall and a road about 20 feet wide. The huge blocks of stone, each weighing almost half a ton, were lifted into place by cranes. In Roman times, the abutment was underwater but the river has changed its course to expose the distinctive feathered tooling and a phallus on the lowest course of the north wing, facing the camera.

MUSEUM AND LODGE GATES

"CHESTERS" HUMSHUCH. 990

CHESTERS MUSEUM Chesters has always been popular with visitors to the Roman Wall. John Clayton, a wealthy lawyer, inherited the Chesters estate and proved to be a devoted guardian of Roman antiquities. *Whenever an estate came into the market, having on it some portion of the Wall, he strove to become its possessor.* On 26th June 1896, six years after his death, members of the Third Pilgrimage of the Roman Wall visited Chesters and saw the hastily arranged exhibits of the new Clayton Memorial Museum. This building is as much a shrine to one man as a collection of Roman remains.

CHESTERS MUSEUM Over the door hangs a fine portrait of John Clayton, whose spirit still seems to preside over his personal collection of antiquities. More than 250 altars, inscriptions and sculptures are displayed in this room. W. P. Collier took several pictures of these solid ranks of Roman stones, all carefully arranged and labelled. The large dedication slab nearest the camera records the restoration of a ruined building at Chesters by the 2nd cavalry unit of Asturians on 30th October, 221 A.D. An earlier slab from the Roman fort at Great Chesters can be seen in front of the fireplace.

The statue in the photograph bears handwritten labels including:

205

3. STATUE OF THE GOD OR RIVER CENIUS OF THE NORTH TYNE. [COLUMN]

4. STATUE OF CYBELE THE DAUGHTER OF THE SKY AND THE EARTH /204/ THE MOTHER OF THE GODS, THE GREAT WORLD-MOTHER AS A FORM OF DEMETER SHE WAS THE SOURCE OF ALL FERTILITY, AND THE GODDESS OF RHEA & AND OF GRAIN AND FRUIT, AND OF ALL THAT SPRINGS FROM THE EARTH SHE HERE STANDS, APPROPRIATELY, UPON A BULL, THE EMBLEM OF AND TILLAGE OF THE EARTH. [COLUMN]

21.

MUSEUM CHESTER'S

CHESTERS MUSEUM   It is probable that this damaged figure was one of a pair. Despite the old inscription on the base, this is a statue of Juno Regina, the consort of Jupiter Dolichenus. Their combined cult originated in Syria and was particularly popular among the soldiers. Juno is shown standing on a heifer while Jupiter would be shown standing on a bull trampling a serpent. Only the base of this statue remains. Even on the frontiers of the Roman Empire, there was a place for fine sculpture. For indoor pictures, W. P. Collier would need to take several shots to guarantee perfect exposure.

9

CHESTERS BARRACKS An inscription found in 1978 confirmed that the Roman fort of Cilurnum was originally built for a unit of 500 cavalry. Each barrack block consisted of eight small rooms, each room housing eight men. The columns that supported a veranda can still be seen. Between each facing pair of barrack blocks ran a street with a central drain. More spacious accommodation for the officer was at the end of each block. This is where W. P. Collier has placed his camera. The stables for the horses were probably built between the barrack blocks and the fort walls.

"CILURNUM" CHESTERS. CHOLLERFORD. NORTH.ᴰ   TREASURE VAULT ROMAN CAMP. 54

CHESTERS PRINCIPIA   The headquarters building consisted of an open courtyard and a covered hall with five small rooms leading off it. The central room held the regimental standards and the other rooms were used as offices. W. P. Collier has taken this picture from the most westerly of the five rooms. The visitors are standing in the covered hall, where the commanding officer would address his troops from a raised platform and dispense military justice. Beneath the arch was the strong room, a late addition to the building, where the remains of an iron-bound oak door were found - but no treasure.

CHESTERS PRAETORIUM This was the house of the commanding officer and the tall pillars of this hypocaust system reflect the quality of his accommodation. The original building consisted of four wings built around an open courtyard. This area was gradually covered over as extra rooms and corridors were added, producing a complicated mass of foundations. The names of officers are sometimes found on inscriptions. Britain was a distant province of limited interest to Roman historians. The excavation of this building in 1843 was the first of many that John Clayton conducted.

CHESTERS BATH-HOUSE The discovery of these remains in 1884 revealed the ritual of Roman bathing. Soldiers came from the right into a large changing room with seven niches. They turned left for the latrines, where seats were placed over a stone sewer. On going up the steps, in the middle of the picture, they turned left for the cold room and right for a very hot room, heated by its own furnace. They carried straight on for a suite of three warm rooms. There was a hot room with a small hot bath next to the furnace at the far end. These remains are in urgent need of careful consolidation.

WALWICK   W. P. Collier has paused outside Little Walwick, which was once an inn called the Royal Oak. The hamlet of Walwick stands on the Military Road, dating from 1752, which for many miles was built on the foundations of the Roman Wall. These could once be seen in the road, especially after rain had washed the dust from the surface, and they may have been visible when this picture was taken. The last chance to examine the foundations was offered in 1928. Road improvements later covered them with tarmac. The people are standing in front of the site of milecastle 28.

TOWER TYE It is thought that Hadrian's Wall was just over twenty feet high, including a rampart-walk and parapet. Over the years, the stone has been used for houses and field walls. Tower Tye was built about 1730 from Roman stones, taken from the adjacent Wall and milecastle 29. In the 1930s, the tower was pulled down to build an extension and part of the garden was removed to widen the road. A fine stretch of the Roman Wall can be seen crossing the fields of Black Carts farm before climbing up to Limestone Corner, where the ditch was left unfinished owing to the hardness of the rock.

LIMESTONE BANK   This stretch of Roman Wall is one of the most popular with visitors, who explore it from the lane that leads past Sharpley farm to Simonburn. In 1873, the workmen of John Clayton discovered Black Carts turret, which measures roughly 11 feet square. Its appearance is unusual because one course of the south wall remains while the north wall is fourteen courses high. The turret was so overgrown by the time of W. P. Collier that he took this picture further up Limestone Bank, where there are fine views and Roman stones still peep through the grass and gorse.

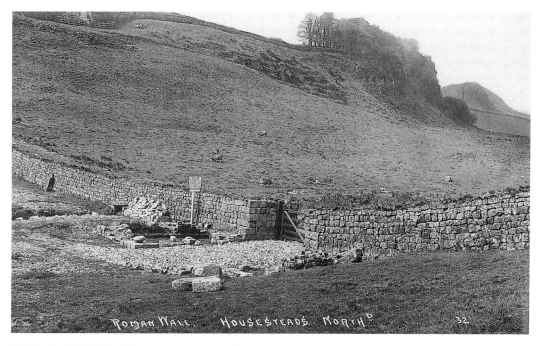

ROMAN WALL. HOUSESTEADS NORTH.ᵈ 32

KNAG BURN   The excavation of this Roman gateway in January 1936 makes this picture one of the last that W. P. Collier took for his Roman Wall collection. It was added in the fourth century to control the passage of locals and traders through the Wall. Two pairs of gates enabled wagons to be stopped and examined before being allowed to continue, probably on payment of a toll. The notice reads "A charge of 6d. each person will be made for admission to the camp. Tickets must be obtained at the Farm House and given up to the caretaker in the camp. Parties of over 20, 3d. each. No dogs allowed."

ROMAN CAMP. "BORCOCIVUS" HOUSESTEADS. NORTH^{D.} I.

HOUSESTEADS PRINCIPIA   The headquarters building consisted of an open courtyard, a covered hall with a platform, from which the commanding officer spoke to his men, and five small rooms. The central room housed the regimental standards and the two rooms on each side were used as offices. This picture was taken inside the covered hall, looking north, with the five small rooms on the left and the platform towards the right. The room in the north west corner was later used as an armoury. The huts date from 1931-1932, when the National Trust cleared up their new acquisition.

CHAPEL OF THE STANDARDS

ROMAN CAMP. HOUSESTEADS. NORTHUMBERLAND. 25.

HOUSESTEADS PRINCIPIA   W. P. Collier did not like people on his pictures but he made an exception for Thomas Thompson (1850-1938) who lived at Housesteads farm for 63 years and was caretaker of Housesteads fort from 1910-1938, first for the Clayton family and then for the National Trust. He himself discovered several important Roman remains and had many stories to tell about the early excavations. He sits proudly among the stones of the Roman fort of Vercovicium, in the room where the regimental standards were kept, at the heart of the headquarters building.

HOUSESTEADS NORTH GRANARY   There was originally one large granary at Housesteads, a prominent building, situated in the highest and driest part of the fort. This single granary was later divided into two separate granaries. There was a loading platform at the west end, furthest from the camera. Granaries are recognised by their strong external walls and buttresses. W. P. Collier was struck by the solid rows of stone piers, which supported the joists of a wooden floor and protected the grain from damp and vermin. Ventilation holes at ground level allowed fresh air to circulate.

HOUSESTEADS SOUTH GRANARY Roman stones peep through the debris, not long before consolidation by the National Trust in 1931 and 1932. In the fourth century, the western half of this granary was converted into living quarters. A post-mediaeval malt-kiln was found to the left of the large stone slab. Thomas Thompson was known to thousands of visitors and was well over eighty when this picture was taken. Born at High Rochester, within the ramparts of the Roman fort, he spoke the richest of Northumbrian dialects and was a zealous custodian of the remains entrusted to him.

BORCOVICIUM" S.E. ANGLE. HOUSESTEADS. NORTHD 13.

HOUSESTEADS LATRINE   A unit of 1000 infantry needed good sanitation and a reliable supply of fresh water for flushing the latrines and for washing. Built in the south-east corner of the fort, at its lowest point, this latrine was flushed by the water that flowed from the nearby stone storage tank into stone channels. The soldiers sat on seats over a stone sewer, now uncovered, and used bracken, moss, or sponges as toilet paper. No Roman wells or aqueducts have been found - but there was no shortage of rain. This was collected in stone tanks, several of which can still be seen around the fort.

"SOUTH GATE" BORCOVICUS HOUSESTEADS NORTH⁰ ③

HOUSESTEADS SOUTH GATE   Most visitors approach Housesteads from the south, though Roman traffic used the Military Way, which ran through the east and west gates. Outside the south gate was the civil settlement and a path led down to the temple of Mithras. Worship involved a series of secret rites. Nothing remains of this temple but a fine example can be seen at Carrawburgh fort. The remains of this gate are complicated because a mediaeval bastle, or fortified farmhouse, was built against the south wall. The eastern guard chamber was later converted into a large corn-drying kiln.

VILLA OUTSIDE FORT. ROMAN CAMP. HOUSESTEADS 29

HOUSESTEADS VICUS Excavations outside the south gate started in 1931 and W. P. Collier took this picture of the civil settlement, where the irregular clusters of buildings contrasted with the planned lines of the fort. Here the soldiers could spend their wages on gambling, drinking and women. For many years, the Roman army did not recognise marriage but relationships developed between soldiers and local women, who would live around the fort. This building was called Murder House because it revealed two skeletons, one of which still had the point of a sword between its ribs.

STATUES FOUND AT HOUSESTEADS ROMAN CAMP. NORTHD. 22.

HOUSESTEADS STATUES   Religion was an important part of military life and the soldiers were expected to follow the official practices of the Roman army and the cults of their own unit. Other beliefs were left to the individual. These three statues were found between 1931 and 1933 during excavations outside the fort. Two statues of Mercury flank three hooded and cloaked deities, called the Genii Cucullati, who were recovered from their small shrine in the civil settlement. Housesteads Museum displays these sculptures and a small number of finds from other excavations.

"EAST GATE" "BORCIVICUS." HOUSESTEADS NORTH.º (8)

HOUSESTEADS EAST GATE Though often overlooked by the casual visitor, the east gate was the main entrance to Housesteads fort because it was on the Military Way, a road that linked all the forts along the Wall. Everyone came through this gate, including messengers and traders, bringing food, news, equipment and pay. Deep wheel ruts in the threshold of the north portal prove the numbers of vehicles that used this route. The ruts are some 4ft. 8in. apart, a gauge that became standard for wheeled traffic. Soldiers also used this gate to visit their bath-house on the eastern side of the Knag Burn.

HOUSESTEADS WEST GATE Roman forts were built to a uniform plan, about five units long and three units wide, with rounded corners, like a playing card. The sixteen forts along the Wall were between three and five acres in size, though cavalry forts were larger. The forts had four gates, one in each of the sides, and six if they projected beyond the Wall. John Clayton cleared the west gate in 1850 and 1851. It is the best preserved of the four gates at Housesteads, since both portals were blocked during the fourth century to form a solid mass of stone that later generations found difficult to remove.

HOUSESTEADS NORTH GATE   John Clayton began excavations of this gate in 1852. The external stone ramp was removed to expose the original foundations and so the road was not as steep as it now appears. This gate has two portals, divided by piers, the inner of which stands to an impressive height. The stone tank collected rain water from the roof. At this point, the visitor can appreciate the harsh conditions that the soldiers of Housesteads faced but the fort was built here to guard the Knag Burn. This was the most popular postcard of Housesteads that W. P. Collier produced.

ROMAN WALL, HOUSESTEADS. NORTH? 31

HOUSESTEADS TURRET 36b This picture was taken near the site of turret 36b. Excavation in 1945 revealed that Housesteads fort was built over the foundations of this turret. It was originally planned to have no forts on the Wall but a series of milecastles and turrets, which the soldiers would patrol from their forts on the Stanegate frontier, a couple of miles south. The visit of the Emperor Hadrian to Britain in 122 A.D. led to the decision to build new forts on the line of the Wall. The remains of a hearth against the north wall of this turret proved that it was used for a short time and then demolished.

ROMAN WALL. HOUSESTEADS, NORTH⁰ 23.

HOUSESTEADS WOOD   The National Trust cleared this area of debris in 1931 and 1932 to expose the fine state of the Roman stonework. A path on the south side now gives a good view of the offsets. The Wall was built in sections about 45 yards long and each section was not always the same width. Roman centurions were in charge of the building and inserted inscriptions to record their work. This grand statement of Roman imperialism has always required constant maintenance - but Hadrian viewed the Roman Empire like a garden, separating what was worth cultivating from what would need greater effort.

MILECASTLE NEAR BORCOVICIUS   NORTH⊙   15.

MILECASTLE 37 Measuring almost 58 feet east to west and 50 feet north to south, with rounded corners, Housesteads milecastle was first excavated by John Clayton in 1853. W. P. Collier took this picture in 1933, after the eastern barrack block had been excavated. It is unclear how many men were stationed here, since Housesteads fort is only 450 yards away. Several stones from the arch of the north gateway have been recovered during excavations. The steep drop in front of this gateway makes it of limited value but the Roman Wall was built to a strict military pattern that did not encourage flexibility.

ROMAN WALL. CUDDYS CRAG. HOUSESTEADS. NORTHD 4.

CUDDY'S CRAGS   No book on Hadrian's Wall would be complete without this famous view. The crags are named after St. Cuthbert, who spent his whole life among the people of northern England, performing miracles and preaching the Christian message, before retiring to Farne Island, where he died in 687. In 1104, his remains found their final resting-place in Durham Cathedral, which was built as a shrine to the greatest of all the northern saints and the patron of the Church in Northumbria. The enclosure in the hollow was built for sheep and cattle rather than Roman soldiers.

RAPISHAW GAP   Here the Roman Wall is cut by the Pennine Way, 250 miles long and running from Edale in Derbyshire to Kirk Yetholm in Roxburghshire. This became the first statutory long distance footpath in Britain on 24th April 1965 - after being suggested by Tom Stephenson in the *Daily Herald* of 22nd June 1935. *There need be no Euclidean line, but a meandering way, deviating as needs be to include the best of that long range of moor and fell; no concrete or asphalt track, but just a faint line on the Ordnance Maps, which the feet of grateful pilgrims would, with the passing years, engrave on the face of the land.*

CRAG LOUGH NORTHUMBERLAND

CRAG LOUGH   The walk between Housesteads and Crag Lough is stunning and W. P. Collier could not resist a sweeping panorama like this. He has taken this fine view of Tynedale from Hotbank Crags, 327 metres above sea level and the second highest point on the Roman Wall. The line of the Wall runs along the edge of Highshield Crags, which overlook Crag Lough far below, and continues along Peel Crags towards Steel Rigg. Hotbank farm lies hidden behind the trees. In the meadow, on the right, the small circles of lighter grass were left after the hay pikes had been led away for winter fodder.

GROWING UP AROUND BARDON MILL

Frances and Agnes Lamb, the daughters of John and Elizabeth Lamb, lived in Primrose House, not far from the village of Bardon Mill. Frances was born in 1900, three years after her sister. Their father was a miner and mother looked after the house and children. This was a full-time occupation without the help of modern conveniences. After her mother died, Frances left Primrose House and moved down to Redburn. She recalls almost a hundred years with great affection.

"I have had a good life and there is not much that I would want to change. I can just remember my baby brother. I was four when he was born but he only lived for a few days. Mother was very ill. The preacher held a service in our house and then laid my brother in a little coffin. My sister and I were dressed in white. The undertaker put the coffin under his arm and carried it down to Henshaw church.

Father was head of the house. It would not be Sunday dinner if he did not carve the meat. When my sister and I had whooping cough, he got permission to take us into Barcombe mine. He put us into the coal tubs and pushed us along the track. The air was supposed to help our breathing. Mother taught us how to cook and sew. We made some of our own clothes but mother usually took the material to a dressmaker. We did not think much about fashion - we wore what our parents thought we should wear. We had to be seen and not heard!

The winters were hard but we had some big coal fires to keep us warm. It was a long while before we had electricity. There was always plenty of home-cooked food, pans of broth and dumpling puddings. We grew vegetables and kept a pig and some hens. If we had any eggs left over, we would take them to Fred Hall. He would stand outside the Bowes Hotel every Friday night. We never knew how much we would get - his prices changed every week!

I started school when I was five. On Monday morning, one of the older boys would go round with a little can and fill the inkwells. If you were lucky, you got a pen with a good nib. Mr. Carrol, the headmaster, taught the oldest pupils. You did not have to do much to get the stick! We were all taught the same subjects but the boys did chemistry while we went to another room to do sewing and knitting. The boys and girls had separate playgrounds. I enjoyed school. Writing was not too bad but it was hard work learning tables and pounds, shillings and pence!

Every summer, Francis Bowes-Lyon laid on a picnic for the local children at Ridley Hall. We were given our tea and a bag of sweets. We saved up all year for the annual church outing to Whitley Bay. We all went by train and Bardon Mill station was crowded. When we were older, we would go to the cinema at Haltwhistle. We were well into our teens before we were allowed to stay out late at night. If we came in after nine, we would look at mother to see how father would react! There were three chapels and two churches near us and they all had social evenings. There were always things going on in Bardon Mill. Once a month, the Women's Institute met on Thursday in the Public Hall. I joined when it started in 1925. On a Saturday night, the men would meet in the Reading Room to talk and read the papers. My father and his brothers played in the Bardon Mill Brass Band. People took the band very seriously. I did a few recitals myself called Tyneside Readings.

The only time I ever went near a pub was when my father was ill. Dr. Glass said that he ought to take some Guinness stout. "I do want you to have it, Mr. Lamb. It will do you more good than anything that I can give you!" One of my cousins kept the Bowes Hotel in Bardon Mill. I would not dream of going into the bar and so I went to the back door and got the Guinness. On the way back, I decided to have a taste. It was the most awful stuff that I had ever had! Fancy carrying that all the way home! So my father forced himself to take his medicine - but he was a Methodist and it really went against the grain!

Every village had a shop, even if it was just the front room of a house. It was the best place to hear the news. At Henshaw, Isabella Ridley had a shop in Croft House and sold everything that you could imagine. Everyone knew her as Bella. If I did not have anything to sew at school on sewing day, mother would tell me to buy some material and make a pinafore. We all wore pinafores in those days. Bella always knew what we wanted because we went past her shop on our way to school. If we had a penny, we would spend a halfpenny on the way there and a halfpenny on the way back. On Saturday night, the children went to her shop for kippers. Esther Snowdon would watch out for us and give us a halfpenny to get her a bloater. She was the oldest person in Henshaw that I can recall. She lived all alone in a little cottage. I do not know what she had for Sunday dinner, but the poor soul could not have had much.

There were several shops in Redburn. James and Frances Cowen had the grocery shop. They weighed out the tea and sugar from big containers. There was no packaging. John Johnson was the cobbler in Redburn House before Ernie Hill took over. He was there for years. Joseph Heslop was the butcher. He kept the meat at the back of his shop where he made the sausages. It was a few years before the Co-op came down from Haltwhistle but it was the biggest shop and took over the grocery when the Cowens left. Edward Brown was the blacksmith at Tow House. He was always very busy, as most people had a horse and cart and all the farmers used horses in their fields.

We went to Forster and Robison in Haltwhistle, if we wanted a nice outfit for Sunday School or a special occasion. They were drapers and mother knew the assistants. Mr. Robison would go round the houses with a bag full of goods. People would buy things from him, as his prices were very reasonable. We bought our hats from the Laidlaw sisters at Riverdale. They were milliners and made really posh hats, with lace and ribbons.

Bardon Mill was a very busy place. Coal from Barcombe mine was loaded at the station and the farmers would take their cattle to market by train. The station-master was James Thompson, a big, smart fellow, who lived in the station house. The two porters had big barrows for the milk churns. Henderson Harding had the village shop. Mrs. Reay had a sweet shop. This became a bakery when William Chester moved down from Henshaw. Luke Dodds ran the post office and sold postcards. The Midland Bank opened in a private house every Friday for a few hours. Mary Pearson had a little shop in Thorngrafton. She sold sweets, pins and needles and little things like that. We always bought our aniseed balls from her.

There were two public houses in Bardon Mill. The farmers went to the Fox and Hounds and the miners used the Bowes Hotel. Many farmers would ride down on their horses and there was space for them at the Fox and Hounds. The horses knew the way back to the farms better than some of the farmers. One fellow would go to the Fox and Hounds every Sunday and get really drunk. He would rely on his horse to take him home. My sister and I would be getting ready for bed when we would hear the horse going past our bedroom window. He would be holding the reins but have no idea where he was going.

Haymaking was an important time of the year and people would go and help out in the fields. The farmers never knew how many people would come - but come they did. If the men had been working down the mine all day, they would enjoy being in the fresh air. And they were strong men! They would get their supper - but that was all. They did not expect to be paid for helping out.

We enjoyed our childhood but it all seemed to pass so quickly! We loved Primrose House, though we were a long way from our friends and we often wished that we lived down in Henshaw. But we enjoyed the friendliness that was all around us. Everyone knew each other and helped each other. It was a different world and life was slower. How times change - but we all have to change with the times!"

HOTBANK, CRAG LOUGH. NORTHUMBERLAND. 22.

HOTBANK FARM   This picture was taken near the site of milecastle 38, where the foundations of the Roman Wall and the milecastle are visible in the turf. Beautiful sunsets make Crag Lough a place of rare beauty in the long evenings of summer. Hotbank farm stands beside the Roman Wall as it descends from Hotbank Crags and turns sharply west to ascend Highshield Crags. The Wall ditch can be seen at Milking Gap on the left. *Nothing is more impressive than the spectacle of the Wall, shorn and maimed as it is, careering over the ridges and ever clinging, as it were, to the naked eminence, which it makes one giddy to look upon.*

CRAG LOUGH NORTHUMBERLAND 12

CRAG LOUGH The central part of Hadrian's Wall follows the line of the Great Whin Sill, a sheet of quartz-dolerite rock, which rises and falls in a series of waves. This view shows Highshield Crags towering above Crag Lough. The Roman Wall ran to the south. All this has gone since William Hutton saw a stretch standing between three and eight feet high in 1801. The National Trust has acquired all the land in this picture. It received Housesteads fort from Mr. J. M. Clayton in 1930 and bought the 913-acre Hotbank farm in 1942. These two properties included 3½ miles of Roman Wall.

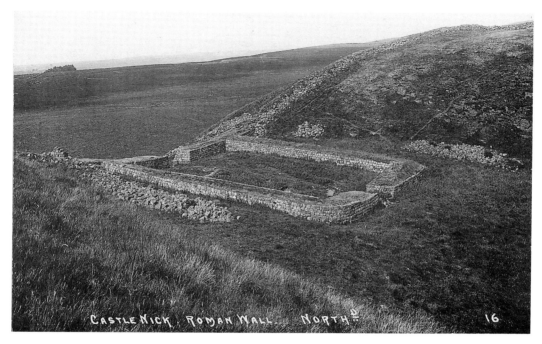

CASTLE NICK, ROMAN WALL. NORTH⁰ 16

CASTLE NICK Measuring almost 52 feet east to west and 62 feet north to south, Castle Nick was first uncovered by John Clayton in 1854. It is one of 80 milecastles that ran the length of the Roman Wall. The foundations of barrack blocks and two gateways can be seen. The recovery of stone dedication-slabs from several milecastles, all bearing the names of the Emperor Hadrian and Aulus Platorius Nepos, a governor of Britain under the Emperor Hadrian, proved that the Emperor Hadrian built the Wall that now has his name, even if many of the visible remains date from later periods.

ROMAN WALL. PEELCRAG. NORTH^D. 38

PEEL CRAGS At the foot of 140 modern steps stands a unique turret, found near the drainage channel on this picture and excavated in 1987. It was built between turrets 39a and 39b to provide greater security by filling in the gap of 767 yards between them. The three drainage holes in the foundations prove the dampness of this area. Peel Crags and Peel Cottage take their name from the mediaeval pele, or fortified tower, that once stood further west. Carl Chard, a local character, was the last resident of Peel Cottage. He lived without gas or electricity and got his water supply from the spring across the road.

ROMAN WALL LOOKING TOWARDS CRAG LOUGH 91

STEEL RIGG   W. P. Collier has positioned his camera to capture the grim determination of the Roman Wall as it strides eastwards along the wave-crest of the Great Whin Sill towards Crag Lough and Hotbank farm. Steel Rigg car park makes this a popular place for visitors to begin their walk along the Wall. It stands on the site of the old farmhouse of Steel Rigg, which was demolished around 1884. Behind the camera is the site of turret 39b, which F. G. Simpson excavated in 1912. The field on the left is where the annual Roman Wall Show takes place on the second Saturday in June.

TWICE BREWED · NORTH ROAD

3246.

TWICE BREWED   The Twice Brewed remains a popular wayside inn and a local guidebook of the 1930s commended *the coolness of its cellars and the mellowness of its amber ale.* The original Twice Brewed Inn is now East Twice Brewed farm. William Hutton stayed the night in 1801 when he walked from Birmingham to see the Roman Wall. On meeting the other guests, he concluded that there was no barricade in their throats and that eating was the chief end of man. After walking the Wall, twice, he walked back to Birmingham and wrote a book. Not bad for a man of 78 years!

ONCE BREWED   This picture is not from the Collier collection but it would be a shame to leave out a view of the original Youth Hostel, which opened on 6th October 1934. Described as a *national hostel for the Roman Wall,* the original building was on the right, beside the busy Military Road. It was used as a byre by Mr. John Ridley of East Bog farm. When he sold it to the Youth Hostels Association, the building was extended to provide accommodation for 40 members. The old hostel was demolished and became a car park after the modern Once Brewed opened its doors on 1st June 1968.

"BOGNOR" MILITARY ROAD. BARDON MILL.   1833.

BOGNOR GUEST HOUSE   Built in 1931 by the Ridley family of East Bog farm, the Bognor soon opened its doors to visitors. In 1933, the AA described the Bognor as offering its members *more modest accommodation for their holidays and on their motoring journeys.* Mrs. Elizabeth Ridley charged her guests the sum of £2 10s. 0d. per week full board, including bath. Now extended and called the Vallum Lodge, this small hotel stands on the line of the Roman vallum, or military ditch, at the foot of Winshields Crags, 345 metres above sea level and the highest point on the Roman Wall.

"CHESTERHOLME" BARDON MILL 1819.

CHESTERHOLM In 1830, the Rev. Anthony Hedley, curate of Whitfield, built this cottage, which allowed him to explore the Roman remains of Vindolanda from his own doorstep. His memorial in Beltingham church describes him as a *skilful enquirer into the history of his native county*. In 1929, Chesterholm and Codley Gate farm were bought by the youthful Eric Birley, whose long acquaintance with this important site led to the foundation of the Vindolanda Trust in 1970. In 1975, Chesterholm opened as a fine museum to display the stunning artefacts found in the fort and civil settlement.

47

ROMAN MILE STONE   CHESTERHOLME   BARDON MILL.   27

CHESTERHOLM This Roman milestone stands in its original position beside the Stanegate, the Roman frontier road between Corbridge and Carlisle. Vindolanda was built around 80 A.D. as one of the forts on the Stanegate frontier. It later supplied soldiers to patrol the milecastles and turrets of Hadrian's Wall before new forts were built on the line of the Wall. No fewer than six forts, wooden and stone, occupied this site and excavations have given a unique insight into life on the Roman frontier. The stone ramparts, which tower over Codley Gate farm, date from the third century.

NEWBROUGH. 1256

NEWBROUGH The church of St. Peter occupies the site of a Roman fort and the village stands on the line of the Roman Stanegate. The elegant buildings reflect the patronage of local families and the wealth from lead mines and stone quarries. The Town Hall was built at the sole expense of Miss Jane Todd of Newbrough Park and was opened in 1878. It is built in the Italian style with a fine pediment and clock over the entrance. The Mechanics' Institute was erected by subscription in 1854 and enlarged by George Cookson in 1890. It has been the home of the Women's Institute since 1948.

NEWBROUGH VILLAGE. 1260

NEWBROUGH Few people of the 1920s had cars and the village shop was vital. John William Nicholson started trading from a wooden shop but built his new grocery store in the late 1920s and ran it until the 1950s. This local character chose a fine location in the centre of the village and sold most things, including petrol at 1/3d. a gallon. W. P. Collier took this picture not long after the shop had opened. It closed in the 1980s, as shopping in towns became the trend. A line of water butts stands outside Red Lion Cottages, long demolished. On the left, the Red Lion Inn remains a popular village local.

SETTLINGSTONES   The Roman Stanegate passes near this old mining village, which once consisted of four stone cottages. A terrace of twelve brick houses was added in 1912. The old West Shaft closed a few years later. Matthew Charlton began his local bus service in 1919 and this was one of the first vehicles that he owned. Until its closure in 1969, Settlingstones mine was the main source of witherite, or barium carbonate, which was widely used in industry and medicine. A 19¼-inch gauge railway took the witherite from the Frederick shaft to the Ellen shaft, further east, where it was processed.

ALLERWASH. NEWBROUGH. 1270

ALLERWASH *The lane between Newbrough and Haydon Bridge passes close to one of the most beautifully wooded reaches of the South Tyne.* The byways of Northumberland are still lined with little gems and W. P. Collier could not resist this view of Allerwash Cottages. The sight of two locals talking to each other simply enhanced the picture of rural tranquillity that W. P. Collier cherished. The four original cottages have been converted into two houses. The taller building in the middle was once an alehouse. The gardens for the cottages were situated across the road, along with their toilets and a pigsty.

HAYDON BRIDGE   Good lodgings and shops made Haydon Bridge a popular venue for tourists in the time of W. P. Collier. The mediaeval village of Haydon was a mile north of Haydon Bridge, where the Old Church served the scattered community. A new village grew up on the banks of the River South Tyne, where the six-arched bridge dates from 1773. A new road bridge opened in 1967 and removed the queues of vehicles crossing the old stone bridge in single file. A continuous stream of traffic now sweeps along Ratcliffe Road. There is a Victorian sulphur spa, a mile east of the village.

HAYDON BRIDGE   Tofts farm looks down on the line of shops in Church Street, named after the church of St. Cuthbert, which was built in 1796 on land donated by Greenwich Hospital, the principal landowner. On the far left was William Urwin, a fishing tackle dealer, the Railway Hotel, managed by John Harker, a draper, a boot & shoe maker, the London Joint City & Midland Bank, a newsagent, a stationer and post office, and a wine & spirits merchant. The shop of Thomas Clemitson, a saddle maker, was on the right. Several of these shops have now become private houses.

RIDLEY HALL   The Honourable Francis Bowes-Lyon (1856-1948) inherited the Ridley Hall Estate in 1888 and turned the old Hall into a fine mansion for his new bride. He moved to Beltingham House when the Army used Ridley Hall in the Second World War. In 1946, Ridley Hall became St. Nicholas' preparatory school. When the school closed in 1966, it became a teacher training college. It now provides boarding facilities for Haydon Bridge High School. Ridley Hall and its grounds are private but can be seen from Allen Banks, where the car park stands on the site of the old kitchen garden.

BELTINGHAM BARDON MILL   1812.

BELTINGHAM CHURCH   As the owner of a large estate, the Honourable Francis Bowes-Lyon built or improved several houses, often adding a brick upper storey. The two cottages near the church of St. Cuthbert carry the inscription FBL 1903. In 1904, he enlarged the churchyard and presented the fine lych gate. About this time, the Bowes Hotel in Bardon Mill was renamed in honour of his family. In 1942, he gave his 185-acre estate of Allen Banks to the National Trust. There are several ancient yew trees and a Roman altar in the churchyard, part of which is reserved for the Bowes-Lyon family.

BELTINGHAM NR BARDON MILL "School" 1817.

BELTINGHAM SCHOOL   The original school was in White Heather Cottage near St. Cuthbert's church. It later moved to Gold Hill, so called because the field that served as the school playground was once yellow with gorse and broom. The cottage on the left was given an upper storey and became the teacher's house while the old byre next door became the classroom. Evacuees from Tyneside swelled numbers during the Second World War but this one classroom school finally closed on 19th July 1968 with just 18 pupils. The last headmistress was Mrs. Margaret Irving, who taught all subjects.

"WILLIMONTSWYKE" BISHOPS RIDLEYS BIRTHPLACE. BARDON MILL 1831.

WILLIMOTESWICK CASTLE The ancestral home of the Ridley family stands on private land but W. P. Collier did not need to stray far from the road to take this picture of the striking 14th century gatehouse. Its most famous member was Bishop Nicholas Ridley, who was burnt at the stake outside Balliol College, Oxford, on 16th October 1555. A cross marks the spot. Of the original house, only two narrow, oblong towers remain, rising above more recent buildings. The Ridleys were a powerful local family and were connected with Unthank Hall, a couple of miles further west.

BARDON MILL

1823.

BARDON MILL   Visitors to Housesteads got off the train at Bardon Mill and people from Tyneside would spend their holidays in the area. Luke Dodds ran the post office and sold his own postcards of Bardon Mill and the Roman Wall. W. P. Collier chose his views to avoid competition and often filled the gaps that others left. There was a Methodist chapel, a reading room, some shops, and two inns, the Bowes Hotel and the Fox and Hounds. Several small drift mines, the pottery and farming provided employment. The Bowes Hotel, village shop and the pottery still remain and the station offers a limited service.

BARDON MILL   The village was named after the woollen mill beside the Chineley Burn. In 1878, the old mill became the pottery of Errington Reay & Co. Ltd., which once made sanitary ware and drainage pipes. The factory now makes a wide range of the finest salt-glazed stoneware, including garden pots, storage jars, chimney pots and ornaments. In 1940, Bardon Mill colliery opened in the field to the right of this picture. It closed in 1973 with the loss of 240 jobs. The narrow footbridge across the River South Tyne is 104 yards long and dates from 1883, when it was built by local subscription at a cost of £553 14s. 6d.

REDBURN   This small village once had a wide choice of shops for local people, including a smithy at Tow House. The village is named after the Red Burn, which cuts under the road near the telegraph pole on the left. A small stone building still houses the village spring. Behind the corrugated iron shed is Floral House, once the butcher's shop, and opposite was the grocery shop of James and Frances Cowen. This became the Co-op, until it too closed in 1971. Behind the trees on the right is Redburn House, where Ernie Hill had his cobbler's shop. One by one, all of these shops have closed.

MAIN STREET. HALTWHISTLE.   3231.

HALTWHISTLE MAIN STREET   Alfred Wainwright visited Haltwhistle in 1938 during his walk along the Roman Wall and his first impressions were not favourable. He described it as a grey town, well past its prime and a victim of dying industry. *The mines are closing, one by one, but still the people linger, as they always do, long after hope has fled.* He found a room at the Grey Bull but not before rain had soaked him to the skin. Several bus operators brought people to the shops and market. One of the earliest was G. G. Ridley, who operated services until a fire destroyed his garage in 1928.

MarketPlace. Haltwhistle. 3230.

HALTWHISTLE MARKET PLACE Every village had a shop but Haltwhistle offered a wide variety - and a Thursday market. This picture was taken outside the old Carlisle Union Bank. The names of shops, some familiar, some half-forgotten, line the street. Forster and Robison were drapers, who were noted for good service and reasonable prices. Mr. Robison would call on his customers with a bag full of goods. Billy Bell & Son still deal in fish and poultry. John Gregg & Sons are still sports outfitters. Graham & Co. were stationers. Bell & Son were chemists: their shop is now the post office.

WESTGATE. HALTWHISTLE.   3228.

HALTWHISTLE WEST GATE   It is hard to believe that this was the main road between Newcastle and Carlisle. All the shopkeepers have elaborate window displays as they compete for custom. W. P. Collier found street scenes frustrating. He preferred landscapes, where he could use a slow shutter speed without the risk of blurred figures - an unwelcome feature found only after printing. He has done well to take a picture without traffic and pedestrians but perhaps he came to this busy town on Wednesday. This was early closing day and the town would be deserted in the afternoon.

HALTWHISTLE BURN The gentle gradient of the old mineral line on the right over the footbridge is a pleasant way to reach Hadrian's Wall. This view was taken near the old South Tyne Colliery, which later became the South Tyne Fireclay Works. Long gone are the industries that once lined Haltwhistle Burn - brewing, tanning, tile making, a couple of woollen mills and the coal mine. The area is now a peaceful haven for wildlife and a popular walk for locals and visitors. The line followed the burn from Cawfields quarry and crossed a fine viaduct on the eastern side of Haltwhistle to join the main railway line.

GREENHEAD   At the bottom of Glenwhelt Bank is Glenwhelt farm, once the Globe Inn, dating from 1757. At the top stood Carvoran farm, once the elevated site of a fort on Hadrian's Wall and now the home of the Roman Army Museum. The Greenhead bypass opened in December 1984 and cut traffic through the village at a stroke. On the left of Greenhead Church is the Greenhead Hotel. In the 1950s, its large gardens were occupied by the caravans of workers at the Spadeadam rocket base. Greenhead once had several quarries and mines and a couple of small drifts are still worked.

GREENHEAD   An AA patrolman stands to warn motorists of the dangerous bend, as they sped down Greenhead Bank towards The Sycamores. This house was a frequent target for vehicles and was finally pulled down in 1952, after a lorry went out of control and nearly killed the Hetherington family. On the right, the Greenhead Hotel proudly displays its petrol pumps. The blacksmith and the reading room were on the left. The village once had a railway station, post office and a Co-op. Greenhead Youth Hostel, converted from the Methodist Chapel, was officially opened on 16th September 1978.

THIRLWALL CASTLE. GREENHEAD. 3350

GREENHEAD   Tradition says that Thirlwall received its name after the Scots thirled, or broke through, the Roman Wall. Built in the 14th century with Roman stones, Thirlwall Castle clings precariously to the hill beside Thirlwall farm. Years of stone robbing have reduced its grandeur. By 1774, some of its walls had been used to build cottages in the hamlet of Duffenfoot. In 1831, one of its walls crashed into the Tipalt Burn. A turret followed in 1986. An inscription, recording building work done on Hadrian's Wall by the British tribe of Dumnonii, has been built into a wall of Holmhead Guest House, on the far right.